CONTENTS

Introduction 5

My Individual Data 7
Name, my location, my kindred, my profession, my nationality, and more

My Health Data 13
Health conditions, insurance policy, main doctor, treatment facility, what to do if I am incapacitated

Important People to Contact 21
Executor, legal counsel, financial planner, insurance agent, medical staff, spiritual advisor

Upon My Departure 27
Who to notify, how to handle the funeral, and details for obituary

My Loved Ones 32
How to take care of them and their details

Vital Documents 36
Last wishes, driver's license, identification card, birth proof, wedding certificate, etc.

Financial Data 40
Legal representative, account locations, cards I use, investments, tax documents, safe box, my debts and credits

Business/Commercial Details 52
About my business activities

What to Anticipate as a Beneficiary 57
Life insurance policies, benefit from your employer, social security, retirement account

Possessions 63
Home, land, business premises, car, family treasures, items of use, gems, lockers, vault, concealed assets

Insurance Options 75
Health, property, vehicle, life and more

Animal Companions 81
Names, information, designated caretaker, guidelines for looking after them

Settle, terminate, and unsubscribe from 85
Services for electricity, water, gas, phone, internet, online and automatic payments, donations, magazines, clubs, library access, etc.

Online Communication and Platforms 95
Credentials for accessing email and social media services, web pages, online journals

Vital Information 101
Things I want care givers to understand when I can't speak, who has access to this book, additional remarks

My Individual Desires 106

Memoir 109
Remarkable moments, milestones

Reflections on Past Positions and Professional Path ---- 113
Facts about my work record

Observations ---- 116
How things have evolved and improved

Reflections on My Life Path ---- 119
My achievements and regrets

Chronicles and Incidents ---- 123
From the people I love, from my home life

My Hobbies ---- 127

My Interests ---- 130

My Passions ---- 132

My Perspective and Viewpoint ---- 136
Political, religious, and societal matters

Well-being and Fitness ---- 140
The care I received for my condition, how my physical capacities have evolved over time

My Travels ---- 144
Top destinations

Lessons Learned from Life ---- 148
My tips for the youth

Closing Remarks ---- 153

Introduction

My Individual
Data

Name

My parents name

Spouse name

Name of Children

My location

My kinship

State

Country

My Profession

Office Address

Office Phone Number

My Nationality

And more

My Health Data

Health Conditions

Treatment

Insurance Policy

Main Doctor

Phone Number

Address

Treatment Facility

Address

Phone number

What to do if I am Incapacitated

Important People to Contact

Executor

Phone Number

Legal Counsel

Phone Number

Financial Planner

Phone Number

Insurance Agent.

Phone Number

Medical Staff

Phone Number

Address

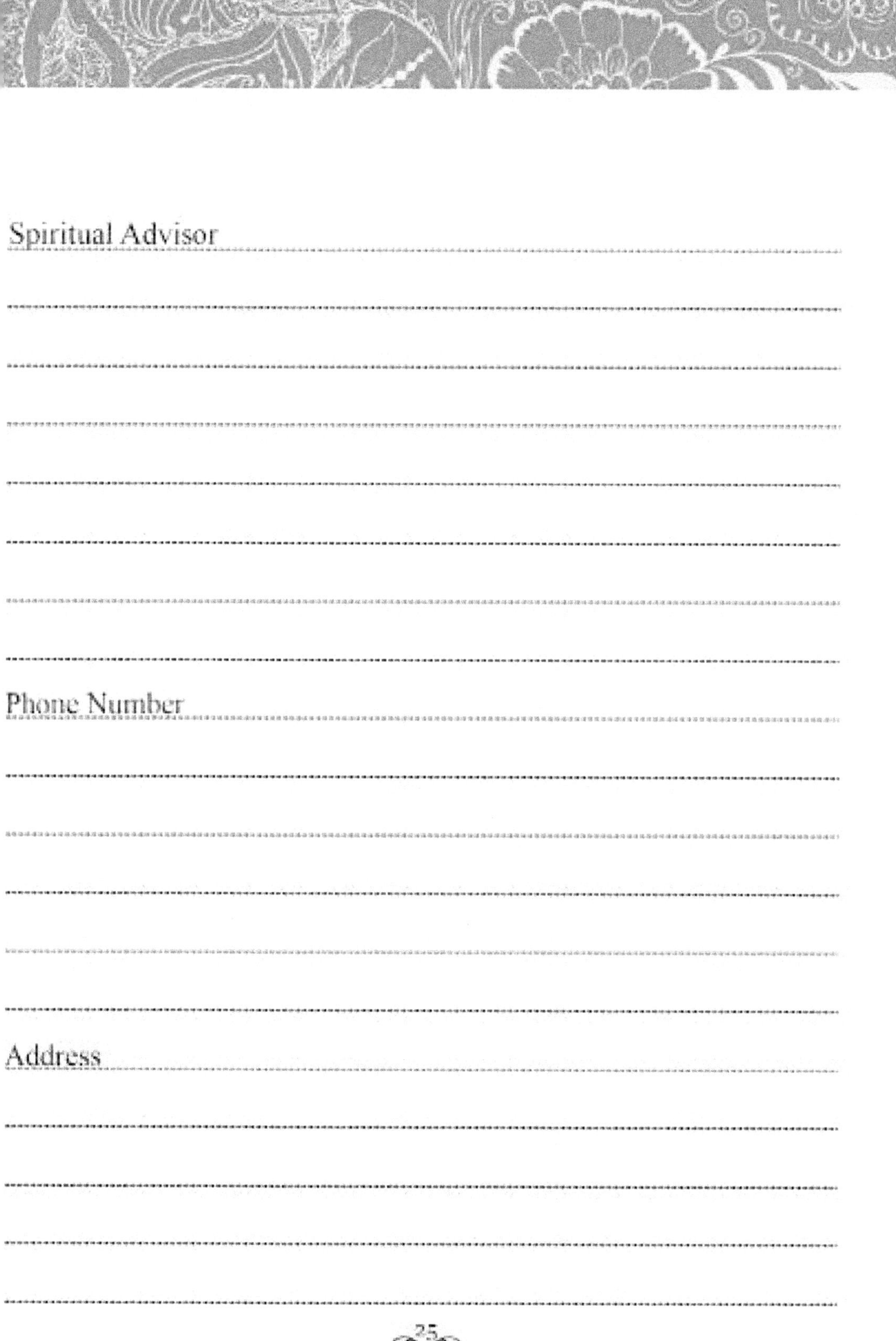

Spiritual Advisor

Phone Number

Address

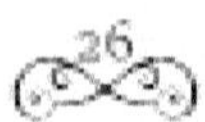

Upon My Departure

Who To Notify

How To Handle The Funeral

And Details For Obituary

My Loved Ones

How to take care of them and their details

Instructions For Their Care

Vital Documents

Last Wishes

Driver's Licence

Identification Card

Birth Proof

Wedding Certificate

Financial Data

Legal Representative

Account Locations

Bank Names

Bank Numbers

Cards I Use

Investments

Tax Documents

Safe Box

Location

My Debts

Credits

Interest Rate

Business/Commercial Details

About my business activities

Location

Staff Strength

Registration Details

What to Anticipate as a Beneficiary

Life Insurance Policies

Benefit From Your Employer

Social Security

Retirement Account

Possessions

Home

Land

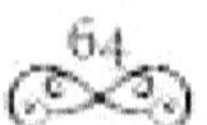

Business Premises

Car

Family Treasures

Items Of Use

Guns

Location

Lockers

Location

Vault

Location

Concealed Assets

Valuables

Insurance Options

Health

Agency

More Details

Property

Agency

More Details

For Rental

For Health

Vehicle

Life And More

Animal Companions

Names

Information

Designated Caretaker

Guidelines For Looking After Them

Settle, terminate, and unsubscribe from

Services For Electricity, Water, Gas,

Internet

Online And Automatic Payments

Donations

Magazines

Clubs

Library Access

Library Name

Online Communication and Platforms

Credentials For Accessing

Facebook

Twitter

Instagram

Snapchat

Email

Passwords for email

Passwords for social media

Web Pages

Online Journals

Vital Information

Things I Want Care Givers To Understand When I Can't Speak

Who Has Access To This Book

Additional Remarks.

My Individual Desires

Memoir

Remarkable Moments

Milestones

Reflections on Past Positions and Professional Path

Facts about my work record

Observations

How things have evolved and improved

Reflections on My Life Path

My Achievements

Regrets

Chronicles and Incidents

From The People I Love

From My Home Life

My Hobbies

My Interest

My Passion

My Perspective and Viewpoint

Political

Religious

Societal Matters

Well-being and Fitness

The Care I Received For My Condition

How My Physical Capacities Have Evolved Over Time

My Travels

Top destinations

Lessons Learned from Life

My tips for the youth

Closing Remarks